EMPLOYMENT TESTS FOR GOVERNMENT, BUSINESS, AND INDUSTRY
SECOND EDITION

TEST GUIDE
AND
EMPLOYMENT MANUAL

DONALD J. D. MULKERNE, Ed.D.
Professor of Teacher Education (Business)
State University of New York at Albany

MARGARET E. ANDREWS, Ed.D.
Former Consultant in Business Education and Placement
Minneapolis Public Schools

Gregg Division
McGRAW-HILL BOOK COMPANY

New York Atlanta Dallas St. Louis San Francisco
Auckland Bogotá Guatemala Hamburg Johannesburg
Lisbon London Madrid Mexico Montreal
New Delhi Panama Paris San Juan São Paulo
Singapore Sydney Tokyo Toronto

Sponsoring Editor: Diana M. Johnson
Editing Supervisor: Susan Goldfarb
Production Supervisor: Avé McCracken/Laurence Charnow
Design Supervisor: Meri Shardin
Text Designer: Eileen Kramer
Cover Designer: Edward Smith Design
Technical Studio: Burmar Technical Corp.

Employment Tests for Government, Business, and Industry, Second Edition

Formerly published as *Civil Service Tests for Typists*

3 4 5 6 7 8 9 0 WCWC 8 9 8 7 6 5 4

Part of ISBN 0-07-043987-7

CONTENTS

TO THE STUDENT

Typists, clerical workers, secretaries, and word processing specialists provide the backbone for accomplishing the great flow of work generated in today's office. They are needed to type or keyboard correspondence and reports, read and check facts or numbers, and sort and file papers.

There are government office jobs available at the federal, state, county, and local levels. In addition, virtually every business and industry employs office workers. Jobs are available in such areas as insurance, banking, retailing, transportation, and manufacturing, to name just a few.

Usually there are more people taking an employment test than there are positions available. People who make the top test scores usually get the first job available. So if you are asked to take an employment test for a government or business and industry position, you should try to do so well on the test that you head the list of those who qualify. That's the purpose of this set of practice tests—to help you head that list.

Test Guide and Employment Manual

Employment Tests for Government, Business, and Industry is divided into two booklets: this guide booklet (Test Guide and Employment Manual) and a set of 16 employment tests (Test Booklet).

This guide booklet contains all the information you will need to complete the 16 tests, score your work, and conduct your own job search. The two parts of this booklet—the Test Guide and the Employment Manual—are described below.

TEST GUIDE

The Test Guide tells you what to expect when you report for an employment test and teaches you how to be test-wise. Before you have completed the 16 employment tests, you will have read each page of the Test Guide several times.

It also contains the general instructions for taking the employment tests, explains and demonstrates the scoring process, and provides you with instructions for using the Progress Chart in the Test Booklet.

Several pages of your Test Guide are devoted to Coachnotes. These are specific hints for each of the individual tests within the 16 employment tests. Some Coachnotes will help you avoid pitfalls commonly experienced by test takers. Others will help you save time or review rules or processes you will need to improve.

EMPLOYMENT MANUAL

The second part of this guide booklet, beginning on page 25, is the Employment Manual. It will help you choose and locate a job, prepare a résumé, fill out an application form, and prepare for a successful interview.

Employment Tests

Of the 16 employment tests, 5 are Business and Industry tests, and 11 are Government tests. Each test is made up of a varying number of individual tests. The longest test, Government Test 15, contains 10 individual tests; Business and Industry Tests 3, 4, and 11 each contain only 3 individual tests. There are 27 different types of tests within the entire set; the most common tests are plain copy typing, arithmetic, and spelling. Other tests are used to evaluate such abilities as filing, coding, using correct grammar, and proofreading.

PART

1

TEST GUIDE

When You Report for a Test

Although the test content for Government tests is somewhat similar to the content for Business and Industry tests, the test setting will probably differ.

GOVERNMENT TEST SETTINGS

Until recently, work in federal, state, county, and local government offices was known as civil service. However, in 1979 the U.S. Civil Service Commission was renamed the Office of Personnel Management. In addition, many state governments have recently renamed their civil service offices. Three commonly used names are the Bureau of Personnel, the Department of Personnel, and the Division of Personnel. Some states now call their government employment exams merit exams.

If you want to take a government employment test, you need to find out when and where the test is given. In some locations, you may simply walk into the Office of Personnel Management and take the test. In other locations, tests are given only on certain dates, and you will need to telephone the office in advance to find out when the tests are scheduled.

The test may be given in a public building, a local high school, perhaps, or an area college. Your desk may be a cafeteria tabletop. If the test includes typewriting, you'll be directed to a special room equipped with various kinds of typewriters. Get there early enough so you can select a typewriter rather than having to take what is left.

Physically handicapped persons who plan on taking the test and who need special equipment should notify the test center in advance. Upon arriving to take the test, make your handicap known to the test administrator, as this may influence where you sit.

BUSINESS AND INDUSTRY TEST SETTINGS

Business and industry tests are usually given under informal conditions. When you visit a company to seek employment, you may be asked to take a test at that time. You'll probably be the only one taking the test, and you will be given time to become familiar with the typewriter you will be tested on. That typewriter may be in the personnel manager's office, at someone's work station in the office, or in a separate examination room. The test may be one prepared by the personnel manager or by the individual doing the hiring, one purchased from a testing company, or a combination of both.

In this program you are to assume that you are applying for a position in five different types of businesses. Each Business and Industry test contains problems that might be included in an employment test given by a specific company. For example, Test 4, which is for the Coast-to-Coast Car Rental Agency, contains chart reading and arithmetic problems. These are the types of problems you might find on a test given by an actual car rental agency.

How to Be Test-Wise

You will probably achieve higher test scores if you use both pretest and posttest time wisely and if you learn how to take advantage of the way that different types of test questions are designed. It is also a good idea to follow basic rules of conduct when in a test-taking situation.

USING PRETEST TIME The following suggestions for using pretest time are for the tests you will take in this program as well as for actual test situations. Use as many of them as you can.

1. Plan to arrive about 30 minutes early for a test. During that time you may have a chance to pick a good location in the room, one that you think may be most comfortable for you. You'll be able to read chalkboard instructions and hear better if you sit up front! Since there may be a number of test takers, you should be prepared not to let distractions break your concentration.

2. Bring with you two sharpened No. 2 pencils, a new ball-point pen, an eraser, and a few sheets of bond typing paper. You will use the typing paper for the warm-up exercise that will most likely be provided before you take the test.

3. If permitted, become familiar with the typewriter you will be using. Practice on the warm-up exercise. Check the tab settings, line space regulator, and other mechanisms you may have to use. If the typewriter is not working properly, request another one. Don't be bothered if other test takers are chatting while you are working. You are becoming adjusted to the typewriter. You want to be ready when the test administrator signals the start of your typing test. You should begin slowly and work up gradually to your normal pace of typing. If you feel your fingers getting tired, slow down your typing speed, and gradually work up to your normal typing speed.

4. Listen to the preliminary instructions given by the test administrator. Many people fail tests because they do not follow instructions.

5. When you are given permission to open your test booklet, check it for completeness. If there are missing pages, unreadable items, or any other defects, signal the test administrator or a proctor. Return the exam, and request another copy. Do this before you begin answering the test questions. Listen carefully to any instructions about where to write your name or identification number.

USING POSTTEST TIME Do not rush to hand in your test before time is called. Some test takers want to be the first ones out of the room. But that's foolish. After you have completed the test, go back over the items you were uncertain of or left blank. You can locate them easily if you have drawn a horizontal line next to the appropriate line in the answer column on the answer sheet. When you have selected your answer, record it on the answer sheet, and be sure to erase that little horizontal line. Follow this procedure for all unanswered items unless a penalty formula is being applied for guessing.

Give your paper a final check to be sure your name or the identification number that has been assigned to you is on it. Without this proof of ownership, you might just as well have stayed home and not taken the test.

TEST-TAKING STRATEGIES Many employment tests, including the majority of the tests in this program, are objective tests. And the most commonly used type of objective test is the multiple-choice test. Multiple-choice items measure your ability to distinguish between incorrect answers, almost-correct answers, and entirely correct answers. If a multiple-choice question gives you part of a statement (called the stem), read it carefully. Then look at the suggested answers. If the correct answer is immediately apparent, mark the appropriate space on your answer sheet. If it is not immediately apparent, first eliminate those answers that are obviously incorrect. Often two of the four choices will be more logical than the others. Then decide which of the two remaining answers is more correct. Be alert for clues such as grammatical construction and the use of the words *always* and *never*.

Test takers often wonder whether or not to guess at an answer. The best rule of thumb to follow is if there is no penalty for guessing, by all means do. You may gain extra test points. In fact, if you are running out of time and will not be able to finish an objective test on which there is no penalty for guessing, you may want to finish marking your answer sheet regardless of the fact that you were unable to read the questions. You will probably pick up a few extra test points because if there are four possible answers, there is a 25 percent chance that the answer you give is the correct answer. If there are only three possible answers, there is a 33 percent chance that the answer you give is correct.

However, sometimes test instructions, including some within this set of practice employment tests, indicate that a penalty will be imposed on all wrong answers. This is done to discourage guessing. The penalty for guessing may range from subtracting the number of wrong answers from the number of right answers to subtracting one-fourth of the number of wrong answers from the number of right answers. When a penalty for wrong answers is in effect, *do not* guess. It will be better for you to leave the item blank.

OBSERVING RULES OF CONDUCT

The rules that a test taker (or *competitor*, the term used on federal exams) must abide by vary considerably but are usually more formal in a government testing situation than in business and industry test settings. It is essential that you pay close attention to the test administrator and hear everything that person announces. Failure to comply may result in your disqualification. Here are a few suggestions:

1. During the exam, *do not talk* to anyone unless it is the test administrator or a proctor. This person will be identified for you.

2. Do not take copies of the questions from the room. You should visit the rest room before starting the test, but if you need to visit the rest room during the exam, request permission before leaving.

3. Avoid borrowing from or lending anything to someone else. Have your own supply of pencils, pens, paper, and erasers.

4. Avoid acting in a suspicious manner during the exam. If you have a physical problem that requires you to stand up and stretch, for example, make this known to the administrator or the proctor in advance.

How to Use This Set of Tests

The sample tests in the Test Booklet provide practice in taking the kinds of employment tests administered by government, business, and industry. Test formats are similar to those you will encounter in actual test situations.

TIME ALLOWANCES

In the upper right-hand corner of each individual test, you are told how many minutes you are allowed to complete the test. Except for the plain copy timed typings, this time allowance begins with reading the instructions for the test and stops when you are through with that test. Reading the Coachnotes in this booklet, proofreading your typing, checking answers, and computing and recording your score are not included within the time allowance.

The time allowance for the plain copy timed typings begins with the signal to start typing and ends with the signal to stop. Time for reading instructions and so forth is not included.

Don't forget! Check the time allowance for each test, and try to complete that test within the number of minutes allowed.

USE OF ANSWER COLUMNS

Each individual test tells you how to record your answers in the answer column. You may have to circle a letter or a number, blacken a space, or write in a word, letter or number. Make sure that you give only one answer for each question. If you wish to erase an answer, erase it completely. Any stray marks on your paper may count against you if the test is scored by machine. If you have to blacken a space for your answer, blacken it completely so that there is no doubt about your answer.

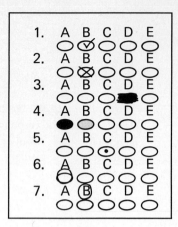

The illustration above shows how *not* to mark a machine-scored answer sheet.

1. Do not use a check mark.

2. Do not use an *X*.

3. Do not blacken outside of the space provided.

4. Do not leave any trace of an erased answer if you change your answer.

5. Do not draw a small dot inside the space provided.

6. Do not draw a circle around the space provided.

7. Do not draw a circle around the letter above the space provided.

By contrast, properly marked answer sheets are shown below.

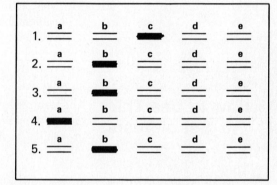

SCORING   Because plain copy or straight copy typing tests are commonly found in both government and business and industry tests, 14 of the 16 employment tests in this program contain such timed typings. The scoring procedure for this type of test is described and illustrated below. You will be responsible for scoring your own plain copy typing tests.

Each of the following seven situations counts as one error for the plain copy typing test, but no more than one error should be counted for any one word. A short paragraph illustrating each type of error follows the list.

1. Any erasure, strikeover, or transposition, or any omission of a word, letter, symbol, or punctuation mark.

2. A space added or omitted.

3. A series of consecutive words omitted, repeated, inserted, transposed, or erased. (All errors within the series are also charged, but the total charge cannot exceed the number of words in the series.)

4. A line or part of a line typed over other material, typed in error in all capitals, or typed with the fingers on the wrong home keys.

```
If you wish to type well, you will need to (tpye) with
                                            ①
control.  This (meansthat) you should not type at a speed
               ②
whereby you (whereby you) make errors.  Of (vpitst,) all typists make errors,
             ③                               ④
but good (typiests) know how fast they can type and (            )
         ⑤                                           ⑥
still retain control.
```

5. Any incorrectly typed word, symbol, or punctuation mark.

6. Any line that has no other errors but extends into the margin so that it is unusually long or stops short of the margin so that it is unusually short. Also, any paragraph breaks that differ from those specified.

7. Failure to follow a specific instruction, such as "Set your left margin at 15." (Some testers will not even score a test if such instructions are not followed.)

The instructions for each timed typing will tell you how to determine the total words you have typed. When you have determined both your total words typed and your total errors, use the Plain Copy Typing Score Chart on page 8 to convert this information into points.

To compute your score, first locate your typing speed in the speed column of the chart. Then refer to column A to determine your speed points. Make a note of these points. Next, refer to column B to locate the number of errors you have made. Follow that line to column C to determine your error points. Make a note of these points. Then, to determine your total points, add your error points to your speed points and divide by 2. For example, if you typed 50 words a minute with four errors, you have earned 3 speed points and 4 error points. For this timed typing, your total points earned are $3\frac{1}{2}$ ($7 \div 2 = 3\frac{1}{2}$).

Your teacher has been provided with the answers to all the other employment tests. If you are to score your own tests, you will be provided with a set of the appropriate answers. Use the scale that follows each test to convert your score into points.

Recording and Evaluating Your Test Performance

Your performance on this set of practice employment tests will be meaningful only if you are able to analyze the points you have earned on the various tests. To help you do this, a Progress Chart is provided in the back of the Test Booklet (page 123) so that you can record your points after completing each test. Then the Performance Graph in this booklet (page 10) will help you analyze your performance.

YOUR PROGRESS CHART

Your Progress Chart will provide a permanent record of the points you have earned on each of the employment tests in this program. Across the top of the chart are the numbers of the tests, 1 through 16. The left-hand column lists the 27 different types of individual tests contained within the 16 tests. It is important to record your scores on the Progress Chart after completing each of the 104 tests. The procedure for completing the chart is as follows:

1. Locate the *number* of the Government or Business and Industry test you are taking at the top of the chart.

2. Locate the *name* of the individual test you have just completed in the left-hand column.

PLAIN COPY TYPING SCORE CHART

SPEED (in words a minute)	A Speed Points	ERRORS	B Error Points
Less than 40	0		0
40-44	1	0	3
		1	2
		2	1
		3+	0
45-49	2	0	4
		1	3
		2	2
		3	1
		4+	0
50-55	3	3 or fewer	5
		4	4
		5	3
		6	2
		7	1
		8+	0
56-60	4	4 or fewer	5
		5	4
		6	3
		7-8	2
		9	1
		10+	0
60+	5	7 or fewer	5
		8	4
		9	3
		10-11	2
		12-13	1
		14+	0

3. Follow the appropriate row and column to locate the box that identifies both the test number and the name of the individual test you have completed. (The correct box should be easy to locate because all boxes that you will *not* fill in are shaded.)

4. Record your score on that test in the appropriate box. For example, if you have earned 5 points on Test 5, Part F (Spelling), you would find the number 5 at the top of the chart and the name of the test, Spelling, in the left-hand column. The white box where the number column and the name row intersect is where you would record your points—5.

5. When you have completed all the parts in any one Government or Business and Industry test, total your points in the appropriate box at the bottom of the chart. Compare your total score with the total number of points you could have earned (also appearing at the bottom of the chart).

6. When you have completed all the tests in the program and recorded your scores on the Progress Chart, total your points for each type of test (e.g., Spelling), and record those points in the right-hand column of the chart. Compare your total score for each type of test with the total number of points you could have earned (also appearing on the right side of the chart).

YOUR PERFORMANCE GRAPH

A graph is provided to help you further analyze your performance on the complete set of tests as well as your performance on those tests that are used to evaluate similar skills and abilities.

The graph on page 10 will provide you with an opportunity to compare your performance on the entire set of tests with the total number of points that can be earned. You will notice that the 16 tests are listed along the horizontal axis and that total points are listed along the vertical axis. The procedure for using the graph is as follows:

1. Review your Progress Chart.

2. Refer to the bottom line of the Progress Chart for the total points you have earned for each test.

3. Refer to the vertical axis of the Performance Graph to find the number of points you earned. (If the number of points you earned is between two numbers shown in the graph, approximate the location.) Place a dot at the point on the graph where the lines indicating the test number and the number of points intersect.

4. As soon as you have recorded the dot for your performance on Test 2, you can begin connecting the dots. The resulting line indicates your performance.

5. Compare your performance line with the line printed on the graph. Wherever the two lines meet or are very close, your performance on that particular test is high.

Coachnotes

The Coachnotes in this section will help you avoid the pitfalls commonly experienced by test takers. Many of the notes contain helpful hints that will help you save valuable time; others will help you with specific skills.

The Coachnotes are arranged in the same order as the corresponding tests in the Test Booklet. Once a Coachnote has been given, it will not be repeated. For subsequent similar tests, you will be referred back to the original Coachnote.

TEST 1: GOVERNMENT

Part A: Plain Copy Typing (page 2). Employment tests for typists almost always include a plain copy timed typing like the one in this test. Some government agencies require a minimum speed for the test to be scored. Some agencies place a maximum limit on errors as well. (See pages 6–7 of this book for a detailed list of errors and an example of scoring.)

Performance Graph

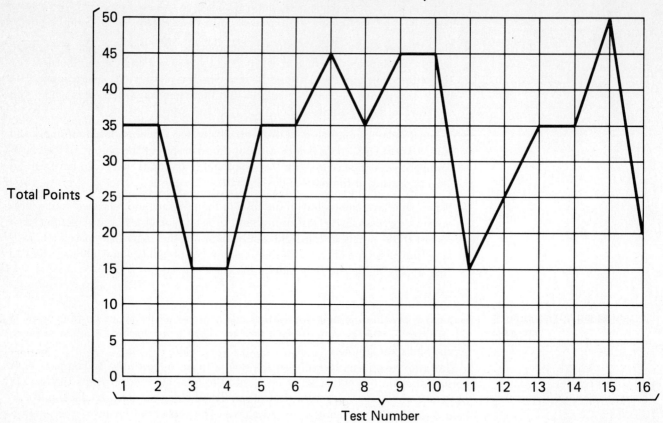

When you take a plain copy test, follow the directions given for adjusting your machine exactly. Determine if you are to listen for the right-margin warning bell, and decide for yourself where to end a line or if you are to copy the material line for line—exactly as it appears in the test.

Use the chart on page 8 of this book to determine your score on this test.

Part B: Letter From Unarranged Copy (page 3). Employment tests often include a letter from unarranged, handwritten, or edited copy. This means that the typist must arrange the letter in a correct style. Before you begin typing the letter, read the directions carefully; they may specify both the letter style and the punctuation style to be used.

Most letters are typed in either *modified-block style* (also known as *blocked style*) or *modified-block style with indented paragraphs* (also known as *semiblocked style*). It is important that you learn these two styles so that you can use them without requesting further instructions. On some tests you will simply be asked to set up a letter in a good style, and you will be expected to follow an accepted style. On other tests the letter style will be specified.

The modified-block style has the date, the complimentary closing, and the letter writer's identification beginning at center. You should set a tab stop at center to save time. The inside address, the salutation, the body of the letter, and the reference notations start at the left margin. An illustration of a letter typed in modified-block style is shown on page 11.

The modified-block style with indented paragraphs is basically the same as the modified-block style. The only difference is that the first line of each paragraph in the body of the letter is indented 5 spaces. An illustration of a letter typed in this style is also shown on page 11.

In both letter styles there are 4 blank lines between the date and the inside address and 3 blank lines between the complimentary closing and the letter writer's identification.

January 15, 19--

Mr. Mark Steinman
856 North Avenue
Peekskill, NY 10566

Dear Mr. Steinman:

Thank you for your interest in our career planning service. As you can see from the enclosed brochure, our organization is prepared to assist you with all phases of your job search, including identifying your career interests, preparing your résumé, writing distinctive letters of application, and practicing successful interviewing techniques.

Our office is open until 9:30 p.m. Monday through Friday for your convenience. Please feel free to stop in and discuss your career planning needs with us in the near future.

Sincerely,

Andrea Dalt
Career Counselor

urs
Enclosure

May 31, 19--

Mr. and Mrs. Walter Amelio
16 Central Avenue
Conway, New Hampshire 03818

Dear Mr. and Mrs. Amelio:

We are greatly pleased that you have chosen to visit New Mexico during your vacation. Our state is proud of its historical landmarks, civic centers, and scenic wonders that visitors have traveled thousands of miles to enjoy.

Enclosed is a packet of materials that may be of help to you. In it you will find information concerning the many places of interest in New Mexico. In addition, the folders included in the packet list motels, hotels, and campsites on our approved list. Rates and fees are also given.

If you have any further questions, please write. We will do our very best to be of service.

Very truly yours,

Clifford Rice, Director
Tourist Information

urs
Enclosure

The two most common forms of punctuation style used in letters are *standard punctuation* and *open punctuation*. Standard punctuation calls for a colon after the salutation and a comma after the complimentary closing. With open punctuation these two punctuation marks are eliminated.

Part C: Arithmetic (page 4).

Because you will probably use scratch paper to work out arithmetic problems, you should check to be sure you copied the numbers correctly before solving any problem.

When adding or subtracting decimals, be sure the decimal points are lined up. For example:

$$
\begin{array}{r}
376.4 \\
+\ \ 2.93 \\
\hline
379.33
\end{array}
\qquad
\begin{array}{r}
79.02 \leftarrow \text{minuend} \\
-\ 8.4 \ \leftarrow \text{subtrahend} \\
\hline
70.62
\end{array}
$$

When multiplying decimals, proceed as you would with whole numbers. After doing the multiplication, add the number of decimal places in the multiplicand to the number of those in the multiplier. Then place the decimal point in the product, counting backward from the right. For example:

$$
\begin{array}{r}
79.6 \leftarrow \text{multiplicand} \\
\times\ 3.02 \leftarrow \text{multiplier} \\
\hline
1592 \\
000 \\
2388 \ \\
\hline
240392 = 240.392 \leftarrow \text{product}
\end{array}
$$

If you have time, recheck your work. The best way to do this is to rework each problem, this time changing the procedure. If it is an addition problem, add the figures in the opposite direction (from bottom to top). If it is a subtraction problem, add the answer to the subtrahend; the two should add up to the minuend. If it is a multiplication problem, divide the product by the multiplier; the result should be the multiplicand. For example:

$$
\begin{array}{cc}
\textit{Problem} & \textit{Proof} \\
\begin{array}{r} 10 \\ \times\ 3 \\ \hline 30 \end{array}
&
\begin{array}{r} 10 \\ 3\overline{)30} \end{array}
\end{array}
$$

If it is a division problem, multiply the divisor by your answer (the *quotient*); the result should be the dividend. For example:

Problem	*Proof*
3 ← quotient	30
divisor → 30) 90 ← dividend	× 3
	90

Finally, notice in the test that one answer choice ends with a plus sign (+). This indicates that one or more decimal places have been eliminated from that number.

Part D: Comparing Names (page 5). Many of the names you will be asked to compare will not be familiar to you. You will, therefore, have to compare them very carefully—maybe even letter by letter if they are unusual names. It helps in comparing such names if you place your left index finger under the correct name in the left-hand column and your right index finger under the name you are comparing in the right-hand column. Names must be *completely identical* to be considered exactly alike.

Watch out for names that are similar—for example:

Peter<u>son</u>   Peter<u>sen</u>   Phil<u>l</u>ips   Phil<u>i</u>ps   Philipps

Ehr<u>hard</u>   Ehr<u>hardt</u>   Frederi<u>c</u>   Fred<u>ri</u>c   Frederi<u>ck</u>

When comparing names, it will help to break them into syllables. For example:

D'Agostino   D'ag / o / sti / no

Part E: Alphabetic Filing (page 6). Remember when working with this type of problem that it is the first three letters of the last names that you have to watch.

Part F: Spelling (page 7). Although there is no penalty for guessing on this test, it is a good idea to go through the test and answer all the questions for which you feel sure of the answers and then go back to the questions you are not sure about. Every time you come to a question you cannot answer, make a *light* pencil mark next to the appropriate number in the answer column so you can find it quickly. (Be sure to erase thoroughly all such marks before you hand in your test!) This mark will also help you avoid recording answers in the wrong places.

If you can identify the correctly spelled word immediately, record the answer and go on. Do not waste valuable time reading the incorrectly spelled words.

Part G: Word Meanings (page 8). If you are in doubt about which of the alternatives to choose, do not guess wildly. Try to eliminate quickly the meanings you know are not the correct ones; you will find it easier to choose between two possible answers rather than four. Read all the alternatives before making a choice; do not be impulsive. Do not linger over any one question, for you may not get through the test. If time permits, recheck your work.

<u>guard</u>ian (one who <u>guard</u>s; protector)
en<u>voy</u> (one sent on a <u>voy</u>age or mission)
inter<u>planet</u>ary (between <u>planet</u>s)

TEST 2: GOVERNMENT

Part A: Plain Copy Typing (page 10). See the Coachnote for Test 1, Part A.

Part B: Letter From Unarranged Copy (page 11). The directions for this test indicate that you are to set your margins for a 50-space pica line or a 60-space elite line (depending on your typewriter). In future tests you may not be given line-length instructions. However, you can determine the correct line length if you can estimate how many words a letter contains. A short letter (75 words or less) calls for a 40-space pica or 50-space elite line length. An average letter (75 to 225 words) calls for a 50-space pica or 60-space elite line length. A long letter (over 225 words) calls for a 60-space pica or 70-space elite line length. It will help you if you become proficient at estimating the length of letters without actually counting the words.

Part C: Arithmetic (page 12). When doing division problems involving numbers with decimals:

If the divisor is a whole number and the dividend contains a decimal, proceed with the division. The decimal point remains unchanged. For example:

$$15 \overline{)\ 45.30}^{\ 3.02}$$

If the divisor contains a decimal point, you must move the decimal point in the dividend as many places to the right as there are decimal places in the divisor. Add zeros to the dividend when necessary. For example:

$$90.36 \div .018 = .018 \overline{)\ 90.360} = 18 \overline{)\ 90360}^{\ 5020}$$

$$\begin{array}{r} 90 \\ \hline 36 \\ 36 \\ \hline 0 \end{array}$$

See also the Coachnote for Test 1, Part C.

Part D: Comparing Numbers (page 13). When comparing numbers, it is especially important to compare them in groups. Group solid numbers (with no spaces or hyphens between the digits) by two or three digits. For example:

79436   79 / 436

Say each group of digits to yourself, listening for patterns or rhythms. For example:

256791-E   *Say* twenty-five, sixty-seven, ninety-one, dash E.

The rhythm will help you identify those numbers that differ. If the digits of a number are separated by a comma, a decimal point, or a hyphen, use the groups of digits for comparison. Be especially careful not to transpose numbers.

Part E: Alphabetic and Numeric Filing (page 14). Be particularly careful when both alphabetic and numeric filing questions are included in the same test. Some test takers are confused when they are required to switch from alphabetic filing to numeric filing and back again. For this reason you may want to answer all the alphabetic filing questions first and then go back and answer all the numeric filing questions.

Part F: Spelling (page 15). See the Coachnote for Test 1, Part F.

Part G: Word Meanings (page 16). See the Coachnote for Test 1, Part G.

TEST 3: BUSINESS AND INDUSTRY (GENERAL PRODUCTS CORPORATION)

Part A: Plain Copy Typing (page 18). See the Coachnote for Test 1, Part A.

Part B: Letter From Handwritten Copy (page 19). See the Coachnote for Test 1, Part B.

Part C: Chart Reading and Arithmetic (page 20). Chart reading is a form of applied arithmetic. On this test you are required to multiply decimals. (See the Coachnote for Test 1, Part C.)

TEST 4: BUSINESS AND INDUSTRY (COAST-TO-COAST CAR RENTAL AGENCY)

Part A: Arithmetic (page 22).   See the Coachnotes for Tests 1 and 2, Part C.

Part B: Letter Composition and Typing (page 23).   The important thing to remember when composing a letter is to type *all* the information *accurately* and *clearly* so that the reader understands the message and does not have to take further action. For example, omitting the time that the plane is scheduled to arrive means that the reader will have to call the airport to find out this information.

Part C: Chart Reading and Arithmetic (page 24).   This test requires you to subtract whole numbers and to multiply and add decimals. (See the Coachnote for Test 1, Part C.) The key to success on this test is careful reading. Be sure to pay very close attention to the left-hand column of the chart and to study the example carefully.

Convert the 5% sales tax to a decimal by deleting the percent sign and placing a decimal point two places to the left (5% = .05).

TEST 5: GOVERNMENT

Part A: Plain Copy Typing (page 26).   See the Coachnote for Test 1, Part A.

Part B: Letter From Unarranged Copy (page 27).   See the Coachnote for Test 1, Part B.

Part C: Arithmetic (page 28).   On this test you are required to add, subtract, multiply, and divide fractions.

When adding fractions:

1. Reduce the fractions to the lowest common denominator.

2. Convert the numerators so that they all have the same value in relation to the common denominator.

3. Add all the numerators, and place the total over the common denominator.

4. Add all the whole numbers (if any).

5. Reduce the answer to the simplest form.

Example:

$$2\tfrac{1}{2} + 3\tfrac{1}{5} + \tfrac{2}{3} = \quad \leftarrow \text{numerator} \atop \leftarrow \text{denominator}$$

$$2\tfrac{1}{2} = 2\tfrac{15}{30}$$
$$3\tfrac{1}{5} = 3\tfrac{6}{30}$$
$$\tfrac{2}{3} = \tfrac{20}{30}$$
$$5\tfrac{41}{30} = 6\tfrac{11}{30}$$

Explanation: First, the lowest common denominator is 30 (all the denominators in the problem divide evenly into 30; there is no number lower than 30 for this purpose). Second, all fractions are converted to contain the denominator *30* ($\tfrac{1}{2}$ is converted into $\tfrac{15}{30}$; $\tfrac{1}{5}$ is converted into $\tfrac{6}{30}$; and $\tfrac{2}{3}$ is converted into $\tfrac{20}{30}$). Third, the numerators are added (15 + 6 + 20 = 41). Fourth, the whole numbers are added (2 + 3 = 5). Fifth, the fraction in the answer is reduced to its simplest form (41 ÷ 30 = $1\tfrac{11}{30}$). Sixth, the reduced fraction and the whole numbers are added (5 + $1\tfrac{11}{30}$ = $6\tfrac{11}{30}$).

When subtracting fractions:

1. Find the lowest common denominator.

2. Convert the numerators so that they have the same value in relation to the common denominator.

3. Do the subtraction.

Example:

$$3\tfrac{7}{8} \qquad\qquad 3\tfrac{7}{8} = 3\tfrac{35}{40}$$
$$-2\tfrac{4}{5} \qquad\qquad 2\tfrac{4}{5} = -2\tfrac{32}{40}$$
$$\overline{\qquad\qquad 1\tfrac{3}{40}}$$

When multiplying fractions:

1. Multiply the numerators to get a new numerator.

2. Multiply the denominators to get a new denominator.

3. Reduce the answer to the simplest form.

4. If there are mixed numbers (whole numbers and fractions), convert them into fractions, and proceed with steps 1 through 3.

Examples:

$$\frac{3}{5} \times \frac{4}{6} = \frac{12}{30} = \frac{2}{5}$$

$$1\frac{2}{3} \times 2\frac{1}{5} = \frac{5}{3} \times \frac{11}{5} = \frac{55}{15} = \frac{11}{3} = 3\frac{2}{3}$$

When dividing fractions, the simplest method is to invert (reverse) the divisor and then follow the instructions for multiplying fractions. For example:

$$\frac{4}{5} \div \frac{1}{2} = \frac{4}{5} \times \frac{2}{1} = \frac{8}{5} = 1\frac{3}{5}$$

See also the Coachnotes for Tests 1 and 2, Part C.

Part D: Comparing Names (page 29). See the Coachnote for Test 1, Part D.

Part E: Alphabetic Filing (page 30). When filing names, compare last names first. Consider them letter by letter. If two last names are identical, compare the first names letter by letter. Remember the rule that "nothing" goes before "something."

Part F: Spelling (page 31). See also the Coachnote for Test 1, Part F.

Part G: Word Analogies (page 32). Word analogies require reasoning. You are asked to study a pair of words that are related to one another in a certain way. You are then asked to study a third word that is accompanied by several alternative words. You must determine which of the alternatives is related to the third word in the same way the first two words are related. For example:

GRAPHITE is related to PENCIL as INK is related to:

a. fluid   c. pen
b. eraser   d. blotter

Reasoning: Graphite is used in *pencils* to make a mark when you write. How is *ink* related to one of the four choices in the same way? Ink is like graphite because it also makes a mark when you write. The pen, then, is like the pencil because it holds the ink. The answer is *c.*

TEST 6: GOVERNMENT

Part A: Plain Copy Typing (page 34). See the Coachnote for Test 1, Part A. Knowing where to break a word at the end of a typing line is important. Usually a word can be divided into syllables according to the pronunciation of that word. Therefore, it may be helpful to you to say the word to yourself to get a clue as to where the word may be broken. For example:

approximate   *Say* ap / prox / i / mate   ap-prox-i-mate

Part B: Letter From Unarranged Copy (page 35). See the Coachnote for Test 1, Part B.

Part C: Arithmetic (page 36). See the Coachnotes for Tests 1, 2, and 5, Part C.

Part D: Comparing Numbers (page 37). See the Coachnote for Test 2, Part D.

Part E: Numeric Filing (page 38). On this type of test you must eliminate immediately as many choices as possible by identifying those numbers that are greater than the underlined number. Then study the remaining numbers that are possible correct answers digit by digit.

Part F: Spelling (page 39). See the Coachnotes for Tests 1 and 5, Part F.

Part G: Word Analogies (page 40). This test differs slightly from Test 5, Part G; however, the reasoning process is the same. (See the Coachnote for Test 5, Part G.)

TEST 7: GOVERNMENT

Part A: Plain Copy Typing (page 42). See the Coachnote for Test 1, Part A.

Part B: Form Fill-In Letter (page 43). Form letters contain blanks for filling in the addressee's name and address so that each letter is personalized. There are also blanks for filling in information that may vary from letter to letter. The typed-in material must be aligned carefully; using the variable line spacer on your typewriter helps ensure this. Follow this procedure to achieve an attractive letter:

1. Count the number of lines you will need for the inside address, and add the 1 blank line between the salutation and the inside address.

2. Roll the paper back (from the salutation) the number of lines you counted in step 1. (If your machine is equipped with vertical half-spacing, be sure to roll back 2 clicks for each line determined in step 1.)

3. Roll the paper back from the point you arrived at in step 2 to determine the point at which you will type the date. The standard format requires 4 blank lines between the date and the inside address.

Note: If you were working with a full sheet of paper, you would automatically type the date on line 15, move down to the salutation, and roll back the number of required lines to begin the inside address. According to standard format, the date would always be typed on line 15. Therefore, the number of blank lines between the date and the inside address would vary depending on the number of lines in the inside address.

Part C: Arithmetic (page 44). See the Coachnotes for Tests 1, 2, and 5, Part C.

Part D: Spelling (page 45). Homonyms—words that sound alike or almost alike but have different meanings and different spellings—can be difficult. This is true especially if you are more familiar with one of the two words than the other. Test takers sometimes are too quick to choose the word they know best. Read each sentence carefully, and concentrate on the meaning of the sentence to get a clue as to which choice is correct. (See also the Coachnotes for Tests 1 and 5, Part F.)

Part E: Comparing Names (page 46). See the Coachnote for Test 1, Part D.

Part F: Numeric Filing (page 47). The instructions for this test differ from those given in Test 6, Part E. Be sure to follow them carefully.

Part G: Word Analogies (page 48). See the Coachnote for Test 5, Part G.

Part H: Grammar (page 49). It may be helpful to read each of the choices to yourself and try to eliminate those that *sound* awkward.

A singular subject must be accompanied by a singular verb. A plural subject must be accompanied by a plural verb. For example:

> She *wants* (not *want*) a new car. (Singular subject and verb.)
> They *want* (not *wants*) new cars. (Plural subject and verb.)
> Both Don and Mike *were* (not *was*) pleased. (Plural subject and verb.)
> Neither Don nor Mike *was* (not *were*) pleased. (Subjects consisting

of two singular words connected by *neither . . . nor* or *either . . . or* require a singular verb.)

Be especially careful when you encounter the words *that*, *which*, and *who*. *That* and *who* are used when referring to people. Use *that* when referring to a type of person; use *who* when referring to a specific person. For example:

> She is the kind of person *that* would succeed in that job. (Type.)
> He is the only person here *who* can speak four foreign languages. (Specific.)

That and *which* are used when referring to places, objects, and animals. *That* is usually used to introduce essential (necessary) clauses; *which* is used to introduce nonessential (unnecessary) clauses. For example:

> Have you had a chance to read the book *that* I sent you last week? (Essential.)
> Our new book, *which* I sent you last week, is on the best-seller list. (Nonessential.)

Another common pitfall to watch out for is nonstandard English consisting of words or expressions that do not follow established grammar rules. Watch out particularly for *double negatives*—expressions made up of two negative words. Such expressions make the statement positive instead of negative. For example:

> I haven't got no money. (Double negative, meaning *I have money*.)
> I haven't any money (*or* I have no money).

Part I: Proofreading (page 50). When proofreading printed copy against typed copy, read the material phrase by phrase. If there are unfamiliar, long, or technical words in the material, it may be helpful to read them syllable by syllable. In other words, you need several reading speeds to proofread: one speed to read short sentences or simple phrases, one speed to read difficult words, and one speed to check numbers.

Get into the habit of using one index finger to follow along in the printed material and the other index finger (or a pencil) to follow the typed material.

If you are a poor speller, you should be aware of it. You will have to compare many more words on a syllable-by-syllable basis than the good speller, and you will have to read at a slower speed.

The most common errors to look for in typed copy are misspelling; transposed letters; incorrect spacing between letters, words, and sentences and before and after punctuation marks; omitted letters, symbols, punctuation marks, or words; and the omission of whole lines of copy.

TEST 8: GOVERNMENT

Part A: Plain Copy Typing (page 52). See the Coachnote for Test 1, Part A.

Part B: Arithmetic (page 53). Some of the problems in this test require that you change fractions to decimals. This is done by dividing the numerator of the fraction by the denominator. For example:

$$\frac{1}{4} = 0.25 \qquad 4\overline{)1.00}^{\,0.25}$$

$$3\frac{1}{2} = 3.5 \qquad 3\frac{1}{2} = \frac{7}{2} \qquad 2\overline{)7.00}^{\,3.50}$$

$$\frac{6}{10}$$
$$\frac{10}{0}$$

Note: To change decimals to percentages, move the decimal point two places to the right, and add the percent sign. For example:

$$.25 = 25\% \qquad 3.5 = 350\%$$

See also the Coachnotes for Tests 1, 2, and 5, Part C.

Part C: Spelling (page 54).   See the Coachnotes for Tests 1 and 5, Part F, and Test 7, Part D.

Part D: Alphabetic Filing (page 55).   See the Coachnote for Test 5, Part E.

Part E: Word Meanings (page 56).   See the Coachnote for Test 1, Part G.

Part F: Punctuation (page 57).   As you work through this test, keep in mind that punctuation marks are used to make the meaning of a sentence clearer. Sometimes it is helpful to think about how you would *say* the sentence; you may get a clue as to where to place the punctuation. Where would you pause while saying the following sentence?

> Speed however isn't as important as accuracy.

You would pause after the words *Speed* and *however* so that the word *however* is set off from the rest of the sentence. Therefore, commas should go before and after *however*.

> Speed, however, isn't as important as accuracy.

Commas are used to set off parenthetical expressions, expressions in apposition, dependent clauses, introductory expressions, and afterthoughts and to separate three or more words in a series or words that may cause confusion. Study these examples:

> I believe, however, that the results are good. (Parenthetical.)
> Lee Brown, our senator, has resigned. (Apposition.)
> If you can attend the meeting, please call me. (Dependent clause.)
> To achieve high grades, develop good study habits. (Introductory.)
> The lecture was interesting, wasn't it? (Afterthought.)
> Please order pens, pencils, and paper. (Series.)
> To Joanne, Marie was a very important person. (Sentence may be confusing.)

Semicolons are used to separate independent clauses and when a coordinating conjunction is omitted between clauses. For example:

> The meeting had ended; however, some members stayed late. (This sentence could also be written as two sentences: *The meeting had ended. However, some members stayed late.* This is a good test for deciding when to use a semicolon.)
> Bill has one book; Mary, two books; and Jo, three books.

Colons are used after expressions that lead to an explanation or a series. For example:

> This is the problem: We do not have enough people to do the job.
> The chairs come in three colors: red, white, and blue.

Apostrophes are used to show possession. Here are some examples:

> I wanted to drive my sister's car. (Singular possessive.)
> The boys' bicycles are in the driveway. (Plural possessive.)
> Toys are sold in the children's department. (Plural possessive.)

Question marks are used to indicate questions. When used with quotation marks, they may go inside or outside the closing quotation mark. For example:

> He asked, "Will you be back soon?" (Repeating someone else's question.)
> Did he say "Will you be back soon"? (Asking a question.)

Exclamation points are used for emphasis. For example:

> Hurry!
> I overslept, but I could not understand why I was late!

Dashes are used in place of commas or colons for emphasis. Here are two examples:

Everyone—even the president—was pleased with the report.
Money—that's all they think about.

Hyphens are used in compound adjectives and compound words. For example:

Today is our company's twenty-fifth anniversary.
We bought ten 15-cent pencils.
The London-Paris flight leaves early in the morning.

Parentheses are used to set off explanatory expressions and numbers or letters in an enumeration. For example:

There were very few people (about 12) at the meeting.
Please send the following information about the meeting: (1) the date,
(2) the time, (3) the place, and (4) the agenda.

Part G: Reading Comprehension (page 58). To do well on this test, you must read carefully. Here are some suggestions:

1. Read each passage twice—first to get the main idea and then to find the one idea that is expressed in one of the possible answers.

2. Watch for words such as *always*, *never*, and other words meaning *all* or *none*. Usually they are clues for eliminating the wrong answers.

3. Know what kind of response you are expected to make. For example, you may be asked to find the answer that does *not* relate to the main theme of the passage. Or you may be asked to find the answer that *definitely* relates to the main theme of the passage.

TEST 9: GOVERNMENT

Part A: Plain Copy Typing (page 60). See the Coachnote for Test 1, Part A.

Part B: Letter From Unarranged Copy (page 61). See the Coachnotes for Tests 1 and 2, Part B.

Part C: Typewriting Skills and Knowledge (page 62). This test provides an opportunity for you to see how much you know about good typing style; it covers all the basic rules you have probably learned in your typing courses. After finishing the test and finding out which statements you completed incorrectly, you should take the time to review those points.

Part D: Arithmetic (page 63). On this test you are required to find an unknown number. You are told that a particular number is a certain percentage of the unknown number. To determine the unknown number, set the problem up as a fraction, and cross-multiply. Then divide the numerator by the denominator. For example:

6 is 30% of what number?

$$\begin{array}{l}\text{unknown} \\ \text{number} \rightarrow\end{array} \frac{6}{X} = \frac{30}{100} \qquad \frac{6}{X} \diagup\kern-0.6em\diagdown \frac{30}{100} \qquad \begin{array}{l}6 \times 100 = 600 \\ X \times 30 = 30X\end{array} \qquad 30 \overline{)600}^{\,20} \qquad X = 20$$

To check your answer, multiply the answer by the percentage:

$$\begin{array}{r} 20 \\ \times\ .30 \\ \hline 00 \\ 60 \\ \hline 6.00 = 6 \end{array}$$

See also the Coachnotes for Tests 1, 2, and 5, Part C, and Test 8, Part B.

Part E: Spelling (page 64). See the Coachnotes for Tests 1 and 5, Part F.

Part F: Comparing Numbers and Letters (page 65).   In this type of test it will help if you work from the figures in the suggested answers rather than from the figures given in the question. For example, compare the figures in answer *a* with the figures in question 1. If they do not match, move on to answer *b*. Continue this process until you have found the match. (See also the Coachnote for Test 2, Part D.)

Part G: Word Meanings (page 66).   See the Coachnote for Test 1, Part G.

Part H: Grammar (page 67).   See the Coachnote for Test 7, Part H.

Part I: Proofreading (page 68).   See the Coachnote for Test 7, Part I.

TEST 10: GOVERNMENT   Part A: Plain Copy Typing (page 70).   See the Coachnote for Test 1, Part A.

Part B: Letter From Handwritten Copy (page 71).   See the Coachnotes for Tests 1 and 2, Part B.

Part C: Typing a Statistical Table (page 72).   To avoid the possibility of copying numbers from the line above or below the one you should be typing, it may help to use a blank sheet of paper as a guide sheet. Place the paper over the page in the Test Booklet so that it underlines only the line you are copying.

Part D: Arithmetic (page 73).   See the Coachnotes for Tests 1, 2, and 5, Part C; Test 8, Part B; and Test 9, Part D.

Part E: Sequencing (page 74).   Sequencing tests are similar to puzzles. You have to use each series of letters or numbers at the left as a clue to find the correct answer. When you find the pattern that is used in the series, you will be able to identify the answer from among the given choices. For example:

e g e i e k

The *e* is a clue because it is repeated several times. Let's look at each of the five possible answers provided for this problem.

m e

This is wrong because an *e* has to follow *k* according to the pattern.

l e

Same problem as with *m e*.

e l

The pattern calls for skipping letters: *i* follows *g*, and *k* follows *i*. Therefore, *l* cannot come after *k*.

k e

Same problem as with *e l*. Also, letters other than *e* are not repeated.

e m

This fits the pattern; *e* is repeated, and *m* follows *k*. This is the correct answer.

Part F: Word Meanings (page 75).   See the Coachnote for Test 1, Part G.

Part G: Punctuation (page 76).   See the Coachnote for Test 8, Part F.

Part H: Reading Comprehension (page 77).   See the Coachnote for Test 8, Part G.

Part I: Coding (page 78). All coding problems involve a coding plan. Study the plan and the example carefully. Determine how the answer in the example was arrived at. Check your first answer with the answer in the example to be sure you have followed the plan. If time permits, check your first several answers by converting the code you arrived at back into its original form.

TEST 11: BUSINESS AND INDUSTRY (BAY PUBLISHING COMPANY)

Part A: Plain Copy Typing (page 80). See the Coachnote for Test 1, Part A.

Part B: Proofreading and Retyping a Letter (page 81). On this test you will have to read the letter carefully for content as well as for misspelling, transpositions, and punctuation errors. Unlike the previous proofreading tests, this test does not have a printed copy for you to compare with the letter.

Part C: Word Choice (page 82). On this test you will have the opportunity to demonstrate your knowledge of homonyms. (See the Coachnote for Test 7, Part D.)

TEST 12: BUSINESS AND INDUSTRY (MIDWAY SAVINGS AND LOAN ASSOCIATION)

Part A: Arithmetic (page 84). See the Coachnotes for Tests 1, 3, and 5, Part C; Test 8, Part B; and Test 9, Part D.

Part B: Proofreading (page 85). See the Coachnote for Test 11, Part B.

Part C: Letter From Handwritten Copy (page 86). See the Coachnotes for Tests 1 and 2, Part B.

Part D: Coding (page 87). See the Coachnote for Test 10, Part I.

Part E: Word Meanings (page 88). See the Coachnote for Test 1, Part G.

TEST 13: GOVERNMENT

Part A: Plain Copy Typing (page 90). See the Coachnote for Test 1, Part A.

Part B: Letter From Handwritten Copy (page 91). See the Coachnote for Test 1, Part B.

Part C: Proofreading (page 92). See the Coachnote for Test 11, Part B.

Part D: Spelling (page 93). Unlike the previous spelling tests you have completed, this test *does* have a penalty for guessing. Read the scoring information carefully before you take the test.

Part E: Sequencing (page 94). See the Coachnote for Test 10, Part E.

Part F: Word Meanings (page 95). See the Coachnote for Test 1, Part G.

Part G: Grammar (page 96). See the Coachnote for Test 7, Part H.

TEST 14: GOVERNMENT

Part A: Plain Copy Typing (page 98). See the Coachnote for Test 1, Part A.

Part B: Arithmetic (page 99). See the Coachnotes for Tests 1, 2, 4, and 5, Part C; Test 8, Part B; and Test 9, Part D.

Part C: Alphabetic Filing (page 100). See the Coachnote for Test 1, Part E.

Part D: Word Meanings (page 101). See the Coachnote for Test 1, Part G.

Part E: Punctuation (page 102).   See the Coachnote for Test 8, Part F.

Part F: Reading Comprehension (page 103).   See the Coachnote for Test 8, Part G.

Part G: Coding (page 104).   See the Coachnote for Test 10, Part I.

TEST 15: GOVERNMENT

Part A: Plain Copy Typing (page 106).   See the Coachnote for Test 1, Part A.

Part B: Letter From Handwritten Copy (page 107).   See the Coachnote for Test 1, Part B.

Part C: Typing an Announcement (page 108).   On this test you will have to center the three-line heading. Center each line in the heading by starting at center and backspacing *once* for every *two* letters (or spaces) in the line. If a letter is left over, do *not* backspace for it.
   Be sure to align the side headings in the announcement at the left margin. Set a tab stop two spaces after the longest side heading (*Eligibility*). After you have typed the first line of item *1*, you will no longer need this tab stop. Instead, reset your left margin at this point, and set a tab stop for the indented lines in the numbered items.

Part D: Arithmetic (page 109).   See the Coachnotes for Tests 1, 2, 3, 4, and 5, Part C; Test 8, Part B; and Test 9, Part D.

Part E: Spelling (page 110).   See the Coachnote for Test 13, Part D.

Part F: Comparing Names and Numbers (pages 111–112).   The directions for the last two parts of this test are unlike those for previous comparing tests. Be sure to read and follow the directions carefully. (See also the Coachnotes for Tests 1 and 2, Part D.)

Part G: Alphabetic Filing (page 113).   See the Coachnote for Test 5, Part E.

Part H: Word Meanings (page 114).   This test is different from those you have completed previously in that you are asked to distinguish between *synonyms* (words that are alike in meaning) and *antonyms* (words that are opposite in meaning). Knowing the synonyms for various words can be helpful when you are writing letters, reports, and memos because you will not have to repeat the same words again and again; this adds variety to your writing.

Part I: Grammar (page 115).   See the Coachnote for Test 7, Part H.

Part J: Proofreading (page 116).   See the Coachnote for Test 7, Part I.

TEST 16: BUSINESS AND INDUSTRY (BRENNAN, MATHIS & NOLAN)

Part A: Plain Copy Typing (page 118).   See the Coachnote for Test 1, Part A.

Part B: Typing a Statistical Table (page 119).   Read the scoring information for this test carefully; it provides clues as to how the table should be typed. (See also the Coachnote for Test 10, Part C.)

Part C: Chart Reading and Arithmetic (pages 120–121).   In Section 1 of this test, you are to use a status table to find the correct answers. Study the table carefully, and determine how it was developed. Then study the example. Check your first answer against the table and the example to be sure you understand the directions thoroughly.

The answers from Section 1 of this test will be used to complete Section 2 of the test, so they must be correct. Read the directions for Section 2 carefully, follow the example, and check your first answer.

Part D: Spelling (page 122). See the Coachnote for Test 13, Part D.

2

EMPLOYMENT MANUAL

"You're hired" are two of the most pleasant words you may ever hear. The employment tests in this program have helped you prepare to apply for an actual government or business and industry job. But there is more to getting a job than taking an employment test. You must also know how to locate a job opening, write a résumé, write a letter of application, complete an application, and perform well in an interview. In fact, in some job-hunting situations you may never get a chance to show that you can qualify by getting a high test score if you do not follow a careful plan for finding and securing a job.

Taking Stock of Yourself

The words *job*, *career*, and *occupation* are frequently used interchangeably in books and articles about employment, but there are definite differences between the terms. A *career* is made up of all the jobs you will hold in your lifetime. These jobs may be in one or more occupations. An *occupation* is a work role, like secretary, computer programmer, or accountant. And a *job* is a position of employment in an occupation within a particular company or institution. The position of typist at Continental Desk Company is a job. It may be the start of a career.

At this time, as you are preparing to find a job, you must choose an occupation or kind of work. Your career will begin with this first job and go on from there to include all your future jobs.

Although it is very unlikely that you will continue in the same job or even the same occupation throughout your entire working life, it is important that you choose your first job and all other jobs carefully. Choosing a job often means compromising, and you should be aware of this. You may take a lower starting salary because of the excellent training opportunities or the chances of certain advancement. You may take a second-choice job because it is closer to home, or pays more, or has hours that fit your personal schedule. Whatever your choice, if it is made carefully, it is your way of starting to build a work record that will continue throughout your work life. Make it the kind of record that will move you along toward success.

Two prime factors to consider when you are trying to find a job are your abilities and interests. If you can find a job that combines these two factors, you'll probably be happier and more successful in the position.

ANALYZING YOUR ABILITIES

For the purpose of this program, assume that you have chosen to work in an office. This should be a good choice because the U.S. Department of Labor's Bureau of Labor Statistics projects that the number of secretarial and clerical *positions* will reach 5.25 million by 1990, with the current average number of *openings* increasing each year to 302,000 in 1990. These jobs represent a wide variety of tasks in a wide variety of companies and government agencies. This means you must check carefully before accepting a job to learn exactly what your job in a particular company or agency will include. Job titles and job duties vary greatly from one office to another.

One reliable way to analyze your own abilities as an office worker is by looking at your performance in the major competency areas included in the practice employment tests in this program. The 27 different types of tests can be grouped into 5 major competency areas.

1. *Typing* consists of the following six tests: Plain Copy Typing, Letter From Unarranged Copy, Letter From Handwritten Copy, Form Fill-In Letter, Typing a Statistical Table, and Typing an Announcement.

2. *Mathematics* consists of the following two tests: Arithmetic, and Chart Reading and Arithmetic.

3. *Differentiation* (of names and numbers) consists of the following three tests: Comparing Names, Comparing Numbers, and Comparing Names and Numbers.

4. *Filing, coding, and sequencing* consists of the following five tests: Alphabetic Filing, Alphabetic and Numeric Filing, Numeric Filing, Sequencing, and Coding.

5. *Language arts* consists of the following ten tests: Spelling, Word Meanings, Letter Composition and Typing, Word Analogies, Grammar, Punctuation, Reading Comprehension, Proofreading, Proofreading and Retyping a Letter, and Word Choice.

Test 9, Part C (Typewriting Skills and Knowledge), is the only test that does not fit into any of these competency areas.

To complete your analysis, follow this procedure:

1. Refer to your completed Progress Chart. Using the scores you recorded in the right-hand column, add up your scores for each of the five competency areas listed above. Record these five scores in the table below.

2. For each competency area, divide your total points by the total possible points. The answer will be your performance rating for that particular area. For example, if you earned a total of 100 points on the six typing tests, your performance rating would be 0.71, or 71 percent ($100 \div 140 = 0.71+$).

COMPETENCY AREA	YOUR TOTAL POINTS		TOTAL POSSIBLE POINTS		PERFORMANCE RATING
Typing tests	_____	÷	140	=	_____
Mathematics tests	_____	÷	75	=	_____
Differentiation tests	_____	÷	35	=	_____
Filing, coding, and sequencing tests	_____	÷	65	=	_____
Language arts tests	_____	÷	200	=	_____

Study your performance ratings to determine your abilities in the various competency areas that office work involves. The scale at the top of page 27 will help you analyze the results.

RATING	EVALUATION
90%–100%	This appears to be a strong competency area for you. You can feel confident that you will be able to achieve acceptable employment test scores in this area and that you will be able to perform well in on-the-job situations.
80%–89%	This appears to be a competency area in which you can perform satisfactorily. Although you may not achieve the highest employment test score in the area, you will probably qualify for employment and perform satisfactorily on the job.
70%–79%	You appear to have some ability in this competency area, but you may need to review some of the employment tests in this program and pinpoint areas in which you need remedial work. You may find it difficult to pass an employment test.
0–69%	It appears that your ability in this competency area is insufficient for employment. You should plan to review the employment tests from this program and do remedial work in this area if you are interested in a job that requires this competency area. It would be wise to plan this remedial work before you risk failure on an employment test.

IDENTIFYING YOUR INTERESTS

There are office jobs everywhere—in big businesses; small businesses; industries; professional offices; city, state, and local government offices; public schools; colleges and universities; hospitals; churches; synagogues; and so on. You are fortunate that as a future office worker you can choose from an extremely wide selection of job settings in many different organizations.

Before you apply for an office job, take some time to identify your own interests. Perhaps you are interested in sports, or carpentry, or dramatics, or stamp collecting. After you have listed your interests, take the time to discover where you might be able to work in an office job that is closely related to one of your interests. For example, if you are interested in camping, you may want to explore the possibility of working in the office of a sporting goods firm. If you are interested in dramatics, you may want to consider the possibility of seeking a job in the office of a community theater.

Of course, there is no guarantee that you will be able to find a job in your locality that combines your abilities with your interests, but if there is one available, you will have a much better chance of finding it if you have taken time to analyze your abilities and identify your interests.

Locating a Job Opening

After you have evaluated your own abilities and interests, you are ready to look for a job opening. It is a full-time job to find a job, so you should be prepared to work at this job a full day every day until you are employed. The first thing you must do is get organized. You will need a notebook, a filing folder, pens, pencils, good-quality bond paper, business-size envelopes, and the use of a typewriter. As you proceed to look for a job, keep a daily record of all your contacts, your research, telephone numbers, and addresses in your notebook. There are several different methods you might use to locate a job opening, and if jobs are scarce, you will probably want to use more than one method. These methods include checking classified advertisements, talking with your school placement counselors, taking a government employment test, registering with an employment agency, and conducting your own job search.

CHECKING CLASSIFIED ADVERTISEMENTS

Most major newspapers and many local papers carry a number of brief classified, or help-wanted, ads that appear in small print. These ads are arranged alphabetically according to occupation. An ad usually gives just enough information to let you know the job requirements and to tell you how to apply. Some help-wanted ads will indicate the name of the company or employment agency placing the ad, while others, called blind ads, will not indicate the company name. Instead, they will ask you to write to a box number. Some ads will ask you to send a résumé, which is a data sheet giving prospective employers information about your work background and education. You will learn how to write and prepare a résumé in a later section of this manual.

When you answer a classified ad, be sure you do it as soon as possible, and do exactly as the ad asks. If it says to write, do so. If it says to telephone during certain hours, do so. And for your own record, be sure to clip the ad out of the newspaper and tape it into your notebook. That way you will be able to refer back to it if you are called for an interview. In most cases you will hear from an employer within two weeks of the time you answer a classified ad. If more than two weeks have passed and you haven't received any communication from the employer, you can assume that the job has been filled.

TALKING WITH SCHOOL PLACEMENT COUNSELORS

High school and college placement counselors are often notified of job openings in the area, and they will help you obtain interviews for these jobs. It is a good idea to begin working with your placement counselor (or guidance counselor) several months before you are ready to begin working, because he or she will be able to help you with decisions about the kind of job you should apply for, the salary to expect, and any additional training you might need.

TAKING GOVERNMENT EMPLOYMENT TESTS

For most government jobs at the federal, state, and local levels, you will be asked to take a government employment test similar to the tests in this program. Those who score the highest on the tests will have the first opportunities to be employed. While other aspects of the job-hunting process, such as your ability to write a good letter of application and your interviewing ability, may be more important in a business or industry job-hunting situation, your ability to do well on employment tests is of primary importance in obtaining a government job.

To obtain information about government testing and employment in your area, call or write the federal, state, and local government employment offices. You can find the addresses and telephone numbers by looking in your area telephone book. Listings might be similar to those shown below:

U.S. Government Office of Personnel Management, Federal Jobs Information and Testing Center

New York State, Labor Department of, Job Services Division, Employment Offices

Westchester County, Personnel Office, Recruitment

White Plains, City of, Personnel Department

If you have difficulty finding the hiring agency at any level of government, call the information number that is usually listed for each level.

REGISTERING WITH AN EMPLOYMENT AGENCY

Employment agencies are organizations set up for the purpose of bringing together people or companies with jobs to offer and people who need jobs. Whenever you read the classified ads, you will probably see that many of them have been placed by employment agencies.

There are two types of employment agencies, state and private. The services of state agencies are free. These agencies handle jobs for many different types of occupations, from laborer to professional worker.

Private agencies operate to make a profit, and they charge for their services. The fee is usually a percentage of the first year's earnings. The fee is sometimes paid by the employee and at other times by the hiring company. Before you sign an agency contract, be sure that you understand the fee structure. If you wish, you can specify that you will accept only positions for which the hiring company pays the fee. These are referred to as fee-paid positions.

One advantage to using a private agency as opposed to a state agency is that there are many private agencies specializing in job opportunities in particular types of occupations. You will probably find an agency in your area that specializes in office workers.

CONDUCTING YOUR OWN JOB SEARCH

One very effective way to obtain a job is to contact employers directly. Use the telephone book or a local business guide to make a list of the companies you would like to work for. Write to them, describing your qualifications. Send them your résumé. (Both letters of application and résumés will be discussed later in this manual.) It is possible that by using this direct approach, you will find a position that has just become available. And if a company doesn't have an opening for you at this particular time, don't hesitate to contact that company again later. Its needs may change with time, and so there may be a job opening in your area within a month or two.

Don't overlook the fact that your friends and relatives may be an excellent source of job information. They may be the first to know about job vacancies in the firms they work for.

Preparing Your Résumé

The fact that you will need to prepare a résumé has already been mentioned several times in this manual. When you prepare a résumé, you have an opportunity, as a candidate for an office position, to show potential employers that you are qualified and that you can prepare a quality piece of office work.

The purpose of a résumé is to gain favorable attention and obtain an interview for you. It is your own personal data sheet that you prepare yourself. It should, of course, put you in the best possible light. Some job candidates prepare a special résumé for each job they are seeking. Others use very good quality copies of one basic résumé. There is definitely an advantage to preparing a special résumé for each job, for you have the opportunity to tailor your qualifications to the specific needs of the employer. However, because it is too time-consuming to prepare a special résumé for each job, most job candidates prepare one perfect résumé and have it duplicated.

While there is no one form to be followed in preparing a résumé, all résumés for beginning employees should contain the same information. This may include your name, address, and telephone number; the position you are seeking; your education, including courses or training that will help you qualify for the job; your typing and shorthand speeds; your work experience; and your activities and interests. You may want to include personal data, but this information is entirely optional. If you have some reason to believe it will help you to include personal data, don't hesitate to do so. Many résumés include the names of two or three references. You may include them, or you may include the statement "References will be furnished on request."

This will allow you to have the option of asking more than three people to act as references for you and using the three most appropriate ones for each job. This technique will also help you keep your résumé up to date because you will not have to change this section if one of your references moves from his or her current address. Study the résumé shown below. You might want to use it as a model when you prepare your own résumé.

Writing a Letter of Application

Whenever you send your résumé to a prospective employer, you may need to write a new letter of application to send with it. The purpose of the letter is to call the employer's attention to those parts of your résumé that are particularly relevant to his or her job opening. If you do not prepare a special résumé for each job you are seeking, you should be particularly careful to write good letters of application.

Traditionally, letters of application sent in answer to a blind ad have used the salutation "Dear Sir." However, since the recipient of the letter may be a woman,

---

MARY JO HEALY
1329 Ravens Road
Akron, Ohio 44313
(216) 555-4357

EXPERIENCE

Factor's Department Store, 483 Main Street, Akron, Ohio
Part-time clerk-typist; January 19-- to present
Responsible for processing credit applications through credit
   agency, typing new account letters and collection letters,
   filing correspondence, and answering store telephone.

Ms. Janice Welman, 351 Westminster, Akron, Ohio
Typist; summers of 19-- and 19--
Typed manuscripts from handwritten copy for textbook author.

EDUCATION

West High School, Akron, Ohio
Scheduled to graduate in June 19--
Business courses included typing (50 words a minute), business
   machines, shorthand (80 words a minute), model office practice, and retailing.

SCHOOL ACTIVITIES

Student Council Member, 19-- to 19--
Secretary of Future Business Leaders of America (FBLA), 19--
   to 19--
Reporter for school newspaper (The West Reporter), 19-- to 19--

SPECIAL INTERESTS
AND HOBBIES

Coaching children in reading through community tutoring
   program, counseling at summer craft workshop for dis-
   abled children, jogging, and playing tennis.

REFERENCES

References will be furnished on request.

```
                                         1329 Ravens Road
                                         Akron, Ohio 44313
                                         May 15, 19--


        Ms. Stephanie Swenson
        Personnel Manager
        Banion's Department Store
        7904 Midway Avenue
        Akron, Ohio 44313

        Dear Ms. Swenson:

             Mr. Robert Sanchez, guidance counselor at West High School,
        has told me that there is a secretarial opening in the personnel
        department of Banion's Department Store.  I would like to apply
        for that position.

             As you can see from the enclosed résumé, I am currently
        working part time in the office at Factor's Fashions.  I have
        found work in the store office to be very interesting, and I
        would like to do full-time office work in a retail store after
        my graduation in June.  Because Factor's will not have a full-
        time opening in the near future, I am applying to other stores.

             I believe that my secretarial training and study of retail-
        ing at West High School, together with my experience at Factor's,
        have given me a good background for the position in your personnel
        department.  In addition to fulfilling my secretarial responsibili-
        ties, if I am hired I would like to learn as much as I can about
        the operations of a personnel department.

             I can make arrangements to come for an interview any day
        after 3 o'clock.  Because it may be difficult for you to reach
        me by telephone during store hours, I will call your office at
        the end of next week to ask for a specific interview date.

                                         Sincerely,



                                         Mary Jo Healy

        Enclosure
```

you may wish to use the salutation "Dear Sir or Madam" when you are answering a blind ad.

Study the letter of application shown above. You may want to use this letter as a model when you prepare your own letters of application.

Completing the Application Form

For almost any job, you will be required to complete an application form. You should always bring the information you will need to complete the application when you go to an employer's office. If you have an opportunity to take the application form home, it is a good idea to make a photocopy so that you can organize your answers and adjust them to fit in the space provided. If you are unable to make a photocopy, or if you are completing the form in the employer's office, use a blank sheet of paper as a practice application. It is particularly important that any application form submitted by a potential office employee be an excellent example of neat, clean, businesslike work.

A sample government application form is presented at the end of this book. You might want to practice completing it as neatly as possible. (Although some of the items on the form would appear only on government applications, private firms would request similar information.)

Preparing for a Successful Interview

If your résumé and letter of application or your telephone call is successful, you will be asked to appear for an interview. This is your chance to sell yourself to your prospective employer. It is important that you prepare yourself thoroughly for a successful interview. This preparation should include selecting the proper attire, locating the company in advance, learning about the company, anticipating questions, and preparing your own questions.

SELECTING PROPER ATTIRE

Select an outfit that will look neat, clean, and appropriate for business. It may be worth the investment to have your best outfit cleaned and pressed for the occasion. Also, be sure your shoes are polished, your hair is neat and clean, and your fingernails will pass inspection.

LOCATING THE COMPANY IN ADVANCE

You do not want to be late for your interview. The best way to be sure that you will be on time is to visit the company in advance. You don't have to go in, but you should make the trip if it is at all possible. You may find the public transportation more confusing than you anticipated, the parking hard to find, or the building itself hard to locate. If you make the trip ahead of time, you will have fewer chances for last-minute surprises on the day of the interview.

LEARNING ABOUT THE COMPANY

Find out what you can about the company or government office in advance. You might ask someone who works there, or you might ask your librarian to help you locate information. You should know what the company makes or does and how large the office staff is. If you can, talk with someone who is already working there to learn if it is a good place to work.

ANTICIPATING QUESTIONS

Be prepared to answer questions similar to the ones presented below. It is your job to sell yourself to the interviewer, so always try to put your experience in the best possible light.

Tell Me About Yourself.   The interviewer wants you to talk about your accomplishments, education, interests, and career goals. You should not talk about your personal life except for indicating meaningful hobbies or interests.

What Courses Do You Like Most (Least)?   Try to describe the courses you like in an enthusiastic manner. Try *not* to show a lack of interest in school. If the courses you like most and do the best in are courses that will help you on this job, be sure to mention that fact.

What Do You Want to Be Doing Five Years From Now?   The interviewer may ask this question to see if you have given any thought to your career goals. You should be prepared to answer it as honestly as you can.

Why Do You Want This Job?   This question gives you an opportunity to show that you have done your homework and learned something about the company. You should speak enthusiastically when you relate the information you have learned about the company.

PREPARING YOUR OWN QUESTIONS

At some point during the interview, you will be given an opportunity to ask questions. If you have some questions prepared, it will indicate to the interviewer that you are interested in the job. However, these should not be only questions about salary and fringe benefits. You should also be prepared to ask such questions as "What are the responsibilities of the job?" and "What are my chances for promotion within the company?"

Interviewing and Following Up

When possible, you should arrange a definite appointment for an interview. Many large companies, however, simply ask that you come in during regular business hours.

On the day of the interview, be at the office on time, and come alone. Say something such as "My name is Jane White, and I have an appointment with Ms. Brown at nine-thirty." You may have to wait, so be prepared to keep yourself busy as you wait patiently.

When you are taken to the interviewer, wait to be greeted. Then say "I'm happy to meet you, Ms. Brown." Don't extend your hand for a handshake unless the interviewer does so first, and do not sit down until you are invited to do so.

During the interview, avoid smoking or chewing gum. Try, if you can, to appear relaxed, but do not slouch in your chair. You have done your homework and are ready for the interview.

When the interview is over, the interviewer will probably rise and thank you. You may be told to make another appointment for an interview with someone else if your interview went particularly well. If you are given no information about what will happen next, you may ask "Can you tell me when a decision will be made about the job?" Be sure to thank the interviewer before you leave.

After the interview, you may want to write a short thank-you letter, but this is entirely optional. If you choose to write one, you can thank the interviewer for his or her time and again explain, briefly, why you feel you are qualified for the position.

Beginning Your Career

As you accept your first job, you are beginning a work pattern that for most people lasts 40 years or more. During those years ahead, the jobs you will choose will determine in large measure the kinds of skills you will develop, how personally happy you will be, the kinds of friends you will have, and even the life-style you will have. Take the time to plan well now to make your first (or next) job a sound building block for the future.

Qualifications Statement

1. Kind of position (job) you are filing for

2. Options for which you wish to be considered

3. Home phone Area Code / Number

4. Work phone Area Code / Number / Extension

5. Sex (for statistics only) ☐ Male ☐ Female

6. Other last names ever used

7. Name (Last, First, Middle)

Street address or RFD no. (include apartment no. if any)

City / State / ZIP Code

8. Birthplace (City & State, or foreign country)

9. Are you a citizen of the United States? If "NO," give country of which you are a citizen.   YES / NO

10. Social Security Number

11. If you have ever been employed by the government, give your highest grade, classification series, and job title.

Dates of service in highest grade (Month, day, and year)
From / To

12. If you currently have an application on file for appointment to a government position, list: (a) the name of the office maintaining your application, (b) the position for which you filed, (c) the date, (d) your identification number, and (e) your rating.

13. Lowest pay you will accept:
$ _____ per _____

14. When will you be available for work?

DO NOT WRITE IN THIS BLOCK
FOR USE OF EXAMINING OFFICE ONLY

Material   ☐ Submitted   ☐ Returned

Entered register:

Notations:

Form reviewed:

Form approved:

15. Are you available for temporary employment?

(Acceptance or refusal of temporary employment will not affect your consideration for other positions.)

	YES	NO
A. Less than 1 month		
B. 1 to 4 months		
C. 5 to 12 months		

16. Are you interested in being considered for employment by:

	YES	NO
A. State and local government agencies		
B. Congressional and other public offices		
C. Public international organizations		

17. Will you accept a job only in your local metropolitan area?   YES / NO

18. Are you available for travel?

A. Not available for travel	
B. 1 to 5 days per month	
C. 6 to 10 days per month	
D. 11 or more days per month	

19. Are you available for part-time positions (fewer than 40 hours per week)?

	YES	NO
A. 20 or fewer hours per week		
B. 21 to 31 hours per week		
C. 32 to 39 hours per week		

	YES	NO
20. A. Have you ever served on active duty in the United States military service?		
B. Have you ever been discharged from the armed services under other than honorable conditions? (You may omit any such discharge changed to honorable or general by a Discharge Review Board or similar authority.)		

C. List dates, branch, and serial number of all active service (enter "N/A," if not applicable).

From / To / Branch of Service / Serial or Service Number

21. Experience: Begin with current or most recent job or volunteer experience and work back. Use an additional sheet if needed.

May inquiry be made of your present employer regarding your character, qualifications, and record of employment?
(A "NO" will not affect your consideration for employment opportunities.) ☐ YES   ☐ NO

A | Name and address of employer's organization *(include ZIP Code)* | Dates employed *(give month and year)* | Average number of hours per week
From   To

Salary or earnings | Place of employment
Beginning $ per | City
Ending $ per | State

| Exact title of your position | Name of immediate supervisor | Area Code | Telephone number | Number and kind of employees you supervise |

| Kind of business or organization | Your reason for wanting to leave |

Description of work *(Describe your specific duties, responsibilities and accomplishments in this job).*

B | Name and address of employer's organization *(include ZIP Code)* | Dates employed *(give month and year)* | Average number of hours per week
From   To

Salary or earnings | Place of employment
Beginning $ per | City
Ending $ per | State

| Exact title of your position | Name of immediate supervisor | Area Code | Telephone Number | Number and kind of employees you supervise |

| Kind of business or organization | Your reason for wanting to leave |

Description of work *(Describe your specific duties, responsibilities and accomplishments in this job):*

22. A Did you graduate from high school or will you graduate within the next nine months, or do you have a GED high school equivalency certificate? | B. Name and location *(city and state)* of latest high school attended

| Yes | Month and Year | No | Highest grade completed |

C. Name and location *(city, state; and ZIP Code, if known)* of college or university.
(If you expect to graduate within nine months, give month and year you expect to receive your degree.)

	Dates Attended		Years Completed		No. of Credits Completed		Type of Degree *(e.g., B.A.)*	Year of Degree
	From	To	Day	Night	Semester Hours	Quarter Hours		

D. Chief undergraduate subjects	No. of Credits Completed		E. Chief graduate college subjects	No. of Credits Completed	
	Semester Hours	Quarter Hours		Semester Hours	Quarter Hours

F. Major field of study at highest level of college work

G. Other schools or training *(for example, trade, vocational, armed forces or business).* Give for each the name and location *(city, state, and ZIP Code, if known)*, of school, dates attended, subjects studied, certificate, and any other pertinent data.

| **CERTIFICATION**
I certify that all of the statements made by me are true, complete, and correct to the best of my knowledge and belief, and are made in good faith. | SIGNATURE *(Sign in ink)* | DATE |